HOPE *for the* FUTURE
from the ONE ABOVE

HOPE *for the* FUTURE
from the ONE ABOVE

❦

JOHN H. GAROT

RESOURCE *Publications* · Eugene, Oregon

HOPE FOR THE FUTURE FROM THE ONE ABOVE

Resource Publications
An Imprint of Wipf and Stock Publishers
199 W. 8th Ave., Suite 3
Eugene, OR 97401

www.wipfandstock.com

PAPERBACK ISBN: 978-1-6667-4592-4
HARDCOVER ISBN: 978-1-6667-4593-1
EBOOK ISBN: 978-1-6667-4594-8

JUNE 22, 2022 4:11 PM

Contents

A DRINKING PROBLEM

Lord, oh Lord, where do I turn?
I try again and again, yet never seem to learn.
To whom can I turn before dying in the urn?
Another arrest and further shame to record.
Where, oh where do I turn, oh Lord?

THE MASTER'S RESPONSE

My son, my son, please strive to learn.
Turn to me in times of stress, and
I'll keep you from getting burned!
Hearken to my word, and I will do the rest.
And provide you with good health and the very, very best!
Amen.

AN UNHEARD PRAYER

There are only two of us on this long, windy road.
When will we have a third, tiny load?
We've prayed and prayed at night and throughout the day.
What can we do to hasten the pace,
Before we can look upon her cheerful, young face?
For us, oh Lord, what can be done, before the final
Setting of the sun?

THE MASTER'S RESPONSE

Your faith has saved you again,
Thanks for avoiding evil and sin.
It won't be long, I assure thee.
Begin to prepare for the days ahead.
And set up a third, very tiny bed.
Because of my grace and your belief,
You'll soon find an end to your present grief.

ANOTHER MARRIAGE LOST

It was painful for us both, from and near,
Neither could see it creeping in from the rear.
No more power left in 'My Dear'!
It's a loss indeed, for all involved:
The children, the grandchildren, and those
Departed up above.

THE MASTER'S RESPONSE

I have tried time and again to veer them away from sin and
    despair.
The bond that the Lord makes can never be repaired.
It is with sorrow, I see this bond broken in two.
Nonetheless, I bestow my blessings upon both of you!

CANCER

Lord, oh Lord, the body is aching and in constant pain.
Will there be relief or forever the same?
I feel totally defenseless and lame.
What can I do and to whom can I turn?
I've read all I can and tried to learn.

THE MASTER'S RESPONSE

Your faith, my son, will save you.
Keep praying and I'll strive to make your body anew!
Life has endless challenges and worries,
But with prayer and thanks, there's no need to scurry.
I'll call upon my Heavenly Father for thee,
And ask that your and suffering will be relieved.

COME HOME, DAD, COME HOME

Wherever thee be, please harken to me.
We all miss you across the wide-open sea.
The war is long over and the firing ceased.
The little one is grown and searching for you.
Come home! Come home! The days and nights are blue.
Day after day, we await to see you back onshore,
With heavy hearts and time-worn lore.
We shall wait and wait forevermore!

THE MASTER'S RESPONSE

My children, I hear your plea.
'Tis not my wish to leave you in pain, you'll see.
Your Dad has crossed the threshold and is safe with Me!
In time, each of you will join him,
And can sit, once again, upon his knee.

COMPANY CLOSED

Lord, oh Lord, what will I do?
The job is gone and employees too!
To whom can I turn for hope and repair?
There is not another company like this very near.
I'm sad, lonely, and in need of faith,
I need your support to find another home for me and my lathe.

THE MASTER'S REPLY

My son, my son. Oh, yea of little faith.
I'll give you all the support you'll need. It's yours to take!
You may need to move and find housing on another lake.
Just contact Me, and I'll return ten-fold because of your genu-
    ine faith.

DEPRESSION

Lord, oh Lord, I've tried, again and again, to do good and avoid
   all sin.
I was sure my reward would lead me ahead.
And guide me to the road home before I am dead.

THE MASTER'S REPLY

My son, my son, do not despair.
I've listened to thee and will answer your prayer.
Very soon, you will see the rewards will come true.
I'll shower you with comfort through and through.
Have faith and believe. I will not let you down.
I'll comfort thee with hope, and with joy, you'll rebound!

DESPAIR

Lord, all around me people are passing, left and right.
Leaving me behind and out of sight.
I need relief, help, and support.
It's time for me to launch my final journey from the nearest
     port.
I'm burned out and feel I cannot take another step.
My body is shot and my dreams are unmet.

THE MASTER'S REPLY

My son, my son, pick up the cross and stay on the path.
Your load is light, and you can make it to the very last.
Continue to pray, each and every day, and help your brethren
     along the way.
Encourage them to slow down and listen to my word.
Within the message is grace and the key to eternal life.
Whatever the problem, look to Me, and I will help you over-
     come the strife.

ENVELOPED BY DARKNESS

Tonight is the darkest night of all.
I can put up my hand and can't even see the ball.
My car is secretly hidden in its own private stall.
One has to wonder if daylight will ever return at all.
This is the moment where faith comes into play.
He promised the darkness would pass and not stay with us all
    day.
It's here for more than a moment. I hope it won't forever stay.

THE MASTER'S REPLY

My son, think back to the joy of spring and fun of summer.
You'll again be able to lay in the hammock and slumber.
It won't be long and night will diminish.
And you'll think daytime will never finish.
That's the beauty of nature and the plan that I've made.
To give man and animals alike, relief from work and the mo-
    notony of day!

FAMILY IS GONE

Oh, Lord, oh Lord, I need your help and support.
I'm depressed and ready to leave life's port.
My family is gone with the wild hurricane.
My life, for sure, will never be the same.

THE MASTER REPLIES

My son, have no fear and never give up your life.
Your family and wife are looking down upon you,
They all wish you well, especially your wife.
Regardless of what happens, I'll always be here to help,
in every way and on-going strife. Amen

FLOWERS IN THE SPRING

Lord, I've tried time and again and again with spade and
    shovel,
To plant the very best and avoid all trouble.
The seeds I've planted, I've watered daily.
And waited for the flowers to flutter in the wind, most gaily.

THE MASTER'S REPLY

Oh, yea of little faith, hope, and dreams.
Look to the skies and pray for some rain.
What I've done for your garden and award-winning beans,
I'll do for your tulips and you'll see the same.
Have faith and it will come to pass.
You'll have award-winning flowers, at last, at last!

GRANDMA, REST IN PEACE

'If only' comes to mind each day I awake.
I pray to God for forgiveness for not spending more time with
    thee before it was too late.
There's no one on earth to take your place.
Each day I pray and hope to you see you again, face-to-face.
I visit your place of rest each and every day,
To beg for forgiveness in every which way.

THE MASTER'S REPLY

My daughter, one day soon, you shall see her again.
Follow the footsteps and avoid all sin.
I have a special place for thee,
Sitting happily upon her knee,
While she signs to thee for eternity.

HOPE BEYOND HOPE

I pray to Thee each and every day, oh Lord.
So that on the final day, I can find the way
To open the gate to eternal life because Thee I obeyed.
I've tried so very hard with all my might.
And continue to follow Thee throughout all my strife.

THE MASTER'S REPLY

My son, my son, very soon eternal life will be yours.
You've obeyed my will and opened all the right doors.
Rather than follow the road of sin and disgrace,
You've found the spiritual path and outpaced many in the human race.
Your prayers have been answered, and eternal peace shall soon be yours.
All you need do is follow the path that leads to the open doors.

I WANT HAPPINESS NOW

Oh, happiness, where art thou?
I've worked all my life and driven straight the plow.
But happiness has escaped me, from the beginning to now.
Tell me, oh Master, what must I do and how.

THE MASTER'S REPLY

Oh, ye of little faith, look beyond self and it will be yours to
    keep.
With a little more work and thought of helping others, sincere
    and deep.
Cross the bridge and take the leap.
Help others and share, each and every day, before you sleep.

JOB DOWN THE DRAIN

Lord Jesus, I've done it again; another job went down the drain.
I'm lost, distraught, and filled with pain.
My life may never be the same.
Which way to turn, what to do, who to see to turn it around?
I truly seek Your goodness, wishes, and comforting sound.

THE MASTER'S REPLY

My son, bear in mind there is but one final judge of all.
What you've gone through is a minor test. Gather your goods
    and stand tall!
Pray to my Father and We shall help you through it all.
It may take some time, but we'll see you through, nevertheless.
Keep the faith, my son, and nothing less.

LIFE IS NOT FAIR

Lord, oh Lord, it's not fair at all.
Jobless and homeless, we're totally stalled.
Over the pain and the loss, we've bawled and bawled.
Where can we turn, what can we do?
How in the world will life ever improve?

THE MASTER'S REPLY

My son, my son, the answer is simple and within plain view.
Open the church door and find a comfortable pew.
Pray to my Father with hope, trust, and love.
He'll provide for you courage and hope to follow the spirit of
    the wonderful white dove.
Prayer is the answer from below and above.
And don't you forget, you have My everlasting love.

LONELINESS

Dear Lord, I feel alone . . . Oh, so very much alone.
I pray to Thee, please bring me home.
My time with brethren has run the course, and I'm prepared
 and ready to go.
Up, up, and away to join my eternal brethren from high and
 low.
Please, dear Lord, let me know your will,
And I'll follow it to a 'T', I will, I will.

THE MASTER'S REPLY

It is with great pleasure I accept your prayers each day.
But your earthly work is not yet complete, I must honestly say.
Continue to share your truth and beauty with all mankind.
It will change you and leave loneliness behind.
Your day will come soon, my son,
But you must continue to maintain your pace and run,
Until the final setting of the sun.
Rest in peace until your work is done!

LOSS OF MY WIFE

She was more than a companion, a mother, and friend.
She gave it her all to the very end.
No sacrifice too much, no challenge too great, it would seem.
She tolerated all, the good and the bad, never expressing a
touch of being mean.
Why, oh why, did she have to go so soon?
'Tis seems we hardly made it to noon.
Just one more sunset, we hoped and we prayed,
But it seems our prayers went unanswered, as under our blan-
kets we laid.

MASTER'S REPLY

My son, my son, grieve not in pain.
She's with Me now and calling out your name.
Soon, you'll cross the threshold and times will be the same.
Hang on and pray to Me and My Father, and Holy Ghost.
You'll soon be united with the one you loved the most.

LOSS OF MY LOVED ONE

Lord, oh Lord, I never knew it could be so very painful and
   lonely, without her on my knee.
Why, oh why, did You my little girl take before her teens she
   would see?
Why not me, with my age and lack of energy . . .
I promised if You were to cure her, I'd be forever faithful to
   Thee.

MASTER'S REPLY

My son, my son, I listened to your prayers and wish for life.
But with the disease, she was on the path of irreversible strife.
I tried my best to intercede on your behalf, but the disease took
   over,
And ended her life just as simple and plain as spring and the
   clover.
Have no fear, you'll see her soon, as soon as you enter the gates
   of eternal life,
And leave behind all human strife.

LOSS OF SIGHT

Lord, oh Lord, I can no longer see Thee.
I can hear your voice, when You return my prayers while pray-
    ing on my knees,
But Thee, I no longer see.
I need Your kind help before this world I leave.
Thee, Who sacrificed His life for all Mankind . . .
Help me, oh Lord . . . Please don't leave me behind!

THE MASTER'S REPLY

My son, My son, your faith has saved you.
Call the church number and you'll find reprieve from the blues.
They'll help with your chores and everyday needs.
You'll have plenty of help before you finally leave.
Thank you for seeking Me out. Your faith has saved you.
Now, I must be about.

LOST CHILD IN BIRTH

My little one is covered with tears.
For years, we've waited and prayed for the very best.
She had everything but the spark of life, nonetheless.
Why, dear God, did You do this to us?
We've prayed and suffered through it all, but that was not
    enough?

THE MASTER'S REPLY

I care for you and truly understand.
You're not alone in this wonderful land.
Pray to my heavenly Father and He will respond.
He'll wash away your pain, all the way around.
Do not despair. Try again.
Continue your lives and remain without sin.
All things will come to pass.

LOST IN THE SAND

Lord, oh Lord, give me a helping hand.
I'm lost and confused in the miles of sand.
Help me, oh help me find my way home.
There's nothing to follow, and I'm totally alone.

THE MASTER'S REPLY

My son, wait for the sunset and walk toward its core.
It will show you the way home and open the door.
Take my hand and hold it tight.
You have my word, you'll be on your way home before it is
    night.

LOST IN WAR

To bad for him and his family tool. The war took its toll and
   he'll never be the same.
He won't survive in society at large; they'll think he's crazy and
   lock him up as insane.
He's not a problem, but a good soldier at best.
Leave it to us and we'll do the rest.

THE MASTER'S REPLY

Why, oh why, do you continue to destroy that which is given
   from the heavens on high?
It's not a game we're engaged in at best.
It's a matter of life and death.
Leave it to Me, the Master on High, and I will assure good
   health and blue skies.

MISSED THE MARK

Lord, oh Lord, where did I go wrong?
Everything lined up perfectly and victory wasn't long.
But, somehow or other, in the final test, it all went wrong
Was I not singing the right song?

THE MASTER'S REPLY

My son, 'twas not your talent nor idea that failed
To cause such panic and unending wail.
I know you tried your very, very best,
But sometimes, it just can't pass the test.
Listen to Me and pray for hope,
To further your life and continue to cope.
Son, you shall see the eternal gate is open to thee.
And peace, joy, and happiness I shall grant, you'll see.

MOM, WE MISS YOU SO

Dearest mother in Heaven above,
If only we'd have treated you with greater respect and love.
We wouldn't have lost so soon, our wonderful, young dove.
When asked to help and assist, we always had to attend first to
    our selfish list.
Now, we have time on our hands, and hours to think
Of how we could have helped straighten the house and empty
    the sink.

THE MASTER'S REPLY

Loving children in despair, weep not for your mom is still near,
Watching you from afar and hoping for the very best,
That all will go your way until eternal rest.
She has loved you well and still does from the day she left her
    cozy nest.

MY DOG IS DEAD

Why, or why, did you leave me now?
I need you more than ever before!
It's hard to walk and I'm severely bowed.
I need your help, my friend, come home.
Without thee, I'm truly lost and alone.
You shall food waiting and a good sized bone.

THE MASTER'S REPLY

Remember, my son, to gain eternal life, one must overcome all
    strife and enter through the golden gate.
It's unfortunate, but Will's time had come . . . Sorry, but it's too
    late.
Look on the bright side and the joy you've had.
Be proud of the good times. Put on your hat once again and be
    glad.
Carry proudly the memories and share them with others.
Listen to Me and I'll keep you from going mad.

MY BEAUTIFUL MOTHER

She was a beauty to behold,
Praised and admired by young and old.
Never once did I hear anger from her,
Only love and respect, as she rocked in her chair.
She looked so beautiful with her bright-colored hair.
Why did you take her, Lord, we were always so near?

THE MASTER'S REPLY

My daughter, fear not, the day will soon come,
After a few more sunsets, your days will be done.
The two of you will be joined once again.
Provided you follow My word and avoid sin. Amen.

MY FINAL PRAYER

I've tried all else. I'll ask Thee just once more.
Dear Lord, help me, before death, I implore.
My life is in knots and my future is dismal.
It seems to be fatal and totally abysmal.
If you have an answer, please share it with me.
So that, once again, a future I can see.

THE MASTER'S REPLY

Open your heart, my son, and listen to My word.
Forgiveness is yours and you'll soon be able to fly with the
    birds.
Open the chest and find the word cope.
Pray to Me, and I'll help you build hope.
You'll see me as a spiritual interlope,
Waiting to fit you with an eternal coat!

MY LAST BREATH

Lord, oh Lord, I cannot go on.
I've failed so often and dropped my baton.
People look toward me with disgust in their eyes.
I can't go on. This is not a lie.

THE MASTER'S REPLY

Oh little one, listen to my word.
All mankind makes mistakes now and then.
Nevertheless, with faith they rise up with the birds,
And react with the positive attitude of 'I can, I can'.
Grab onto that theme, and don't let go.
Look upward to the heavens for the sake of your soul . . .
For the sake of your soul.

MY LYNN IS GONE

Lord, oh Lord, what have Thee done?
Last week I lost my loved one before the setting of the sun.
Our hope, dreams and aspirations are gone.
No longer will we ever sing another happy song.
What is it I've done to deserve such a loss?
I wish it were I and not she I lost.

THE MASTER'S REPLY

Have faith, young man, have faith!
She's looking down upon you in her new chosen place.
Beside her is comfort and joy, outlined in lace.
She's waiting for thee to join her again.
So please move onward and stay free of sin.
It's only a matter of time, and you'll again be with your Lynn.

OH HELP ME GROW

Oh, Lord, from heaven on high,
I need your help to nurture my crops from the mighty sky.
However hard I try and whatever I do,
I seem to miss the mark, through and through.
To Thee, I turn in open prayer and hope,
Begging for You to help me and my crops to cope.

THE MASTER'S REPLY

Fear not, my son. I hear you clearly.
Your hope and wishes will be attended to dearly.
Soon the skies will reply in an abundance of showers
To enhance your crops, as well as your flowers.
Your faith has saved you, time and again.
Continue to pray and avoid all sin.
Soon, very soon, disaster will be a has been!

OVERWHELMING FEAR

Lord, oh Lord, I know not what to do.
I fear to stay and am terrified to go.
I've got another case of the 'blues'.
I beg of You, provide me with help and as a sense of direction,
So that I can get my life moving with a little correction.
If anyone has the gift of hope, it is Thee, oh Lord!
I'll do whatever You command to maintain accord.

THE MASTER'S REPLY

Heed not, my son. I'm here, not gone.
I'll be here to help thee, forever long.
Just pray to Me and My Father above.
We'll harken at once and share Our love.
Your prayers are like music to the ear.
Please keep them coming, year after year!

PRAISE TO THE COOK

Between the tears and the years, she's found the magic.
No more over-cooked meals and no more tragic.
She starts with an apron, and, within a whisp or two,
She's got the job done and ready for you.
She puts the pros to shame at their very own game.
And never presents a meal that is lame.

THE MASTER'S REPLY

'Tis I that directed the young soul from within.
She's free from all sin and past has-beens.
Her talents, I've given to share with all,
Short, medium, and tall, that's all.
The joy that she shares is just a touch of leaven,
Compared to the happiness she'll find in heaven.

RIGHT OR WRONG

Whatever the song, is it right or wrong?
Should I sing with depth and meaning in every song?
Is my mission to entertain or personal wealth to gain?
Within my inner being, I feel such pain.
As I go on stage, night after night, it will never be the same.

THE MASTER'S REPLY

My daughter, take my hand and walk beside me.
Joy, happiness, and success will be there for thee.
With faith and hope comes the strength to cope.
Have no fear, you have miles to go, before you hit the final note.
From now, 'til then, you'll be able to share love, joy, and
        happiness,
Far greater than most.

SCHOLASTIC FAILURE

Another course down the drain,
I think I'm way off track and going insane.
Is there any hope for the mentally lame?
I'm afraid to go home and report the bad news.
They'll only tighten the belt and apply the screws.

THE MASTER'S REPLY

My daughter, have no fear.
Regardless of failure, I'm always here.
I'll help you through thick and thin,
So long as you stay clean and out of sin.
Hearken to my call and I shall save you again.
One course is only a blip in the walk.
Have no fear, so long as we can continue to talk.

SUICIDE

Death is the answer, the only way to go.
I've prayed and shouted for help,
But am leaving as an empty soul!
I've tried again and again to achieve and believe,
But no one would trust me and told me to leave.
My ideas were inadequate and my life a mess.
'Tis time to call it quits and achieve eternal rest.

THE MASTER'S REPLY

Do not despair oh little one, my dear.
There's help from the front and more from the rear.
It goes as far back as your childhood days,
When your Dad would pull you along in that worn-out sleigh.
You'd laugh and you'd sing in harmony together.
In spite of the cold and uncomfortable weather.
Be not so foolish as to take your life.
You've been a wonderful Mother and an outstanding wife!

THE ACCIDENT

The night it was pitch black and shrouded in darkness at every
    turn.
'Twas a night we've never forgotten and will forever recall.
I pulled to the left and pulled to the right.
Just seconds too late to avoid the god-awful site.
In a moment of terror, the body collapsed,
And practically landed on our front seat laps.
I screamed and broke into tears . . .
I'm far too young for this to happen in all my years.
We tried everything to rekindle her life,
But it was all for naught and not very nice.
The ambulance came and took her away.
I felt as if my life was at bay.

THE MASTER'S REPLY

The Lord has given you sun for the morn,
And the moon at night to be careful and forlorn.
Take advantage of the day, and rest in the twilight,
So that the horrors of yesterday will fade with the sight.
Honor and praise the gift of life given,
And pray and work your way toward heaven.
My Father and I will have a place for you,
But you must learn to obey and drive carefully when the skies
    are blue.

THE AUTO CRASH

We told him not to drive tonight.
The fog blocked everything from one's sight.
Around the curve came flying a madman going full speed.
You never had time to avoid the crash and take the lead.
It's now with bitterness, anger, and hope,
We gather together at the bottom of the slope.
And pray no one else comes that way,
In darkness, mist, and an invisible way.

THE MASTER'S REPLY

Beware of nature wherever you be,
There's little hope beyond hope when one cannot see.
I suggest you consider turning off the key.
And return inside where you are safe,
Away from the fog . . .
And comfortable beside the sleeping dog.

THE DEGREE IS IN SIGHT

I've worked so hard throughout the year,
And often shed many, many tears.
I swore each course be my last,
For fear of failure and lack of brass!
Now, I know the degree is in sight.
Someone above turned on the light,
And helped me through to that which is right.
I'm not worthy nor deserving of praise,
From anyone, I've met over the past many days.

THE MASTER REPLIES

My daughter, put on your gown with pride and might!
At last, you'll be honored for all your hard work tonight.
Not many have climbed the hill you've mastered and left
     behind,
Like the American eagle who flies above all mankind.
With degree in hand, you can now proudly stand!

THE FINAL ARGUMENT

I'm right, you're wrong. It's gotten to be a song.
How in the world of the finite word, again and again, can I be
    wrong?
Rather than complain and feel threatened for life,
Please join me, as once you did, as husband and wife.

THE MASTER'S REPLY

It seems the bliss has varnished, and the gold tarnished.
Turn to Me, and I will restore your lives and return your
    harmony.
Don't turn from Me and embrace sin, you'll be forever lonely.
Turn to me and the two of you will win!

THE FIRE

Oh Lord, why did you destroy my home?
Not a thing left, and now we're alone!
Where do we start and to whom do we turn?
Through the years, I've learned a lot, but never thought all
    would be burned.
Tomorrow, it will be gone when the dumpster comes
To haul, trip after trip until it's all done.
How many sunsets will it take,
Before we can go on living on this little lake?

THE MASTER'S REPLY

My son, do not despair,
Your faith has saved you from far and near.
I wish not evil upon you or your family.
Seek out help and, in time, full recovery you'll see.
I don't destroy but help and assist.
Keep the faith and you'll forever be on my list!

THE HOUSE IS GONE

Dear Lord, how can this be, such a beautiful day, and all is lost.
Why have I been burdened with such a tremendous cost?
The insurance won't pay because of neglect.
I have no money for repairs, and nothing left.
Where, or where can I find reprieve and a helping hand?
I need your help, oh Lord, I can hardly stand.

THE MASTER'S REPLY

My son, do not run. Help is on the way.
Call the Christian News and ask for help and a place to stay.
The power of the Lord will be with you today and everyday.
Cast away sin and all thoughts of reprieve.
I'll help you every which way I can, before the earth you leave.

THE JOY OF SUCCESS

Oh Lord, where do I turn, what must I do to achieve success
  and joy?
My burden seems so heavy, yet I'm just a boy.
Why can't I hit the home runs and run the bases?
And share in the joy of winning the race?
Why, oh Lord, why, I ask of Thee . . .
Show me the way, and I shall forever faithful be.

THE MASTER'S REPLY

My son, look not for victory around every corner of the block,
But rather your faith in Me and I shall open the lock.
Life is not a game of win and lose,
But rather a trail of improvement through prayer and sacrifice.
So that, at time of death, you can proclaim,
'Twas not for naught, nor for fame!

THE LAST SHOT

I've been trained through and through,
As a hunter of man and beast,
To aim and hit the mark, time after time, at least.
But the thrill is gone and the eye not so straight.
I've thought of taking my life, as of late.

THE MASTER'S REPLY

My son, there are many behind that rely upon your kind.
You must continue to provide support and goodwill.
There's no longer a need to raise the weapon and kill.
Live out your days in peace and goodwill.
Be kind, considerate, and pray harder, even still!

THE OLD OAK TREE

As truth is God, and God is truth, I bend my knee to Thee.
You've seen us through thick and thin,
Always trying to beat the other for the final win.
You've stood tall and strong above the ground,
Shading everyone, whatever comes around.
It matters not if the winds blow and the flakes fall.
Your outstretched arms continue to safeguard us all.

THE MASTER'S REPLY

Why must you destroy what has given you so much joy?
God's hands have formed a beautiful tree for thee.
Now you think it's no more than a toy.
How, I ask, can you cut down such a beautiful tree beside the
    sea?
It's with a heavy heart and great sorrow, I shall remember thee,
For all eternity, for all eternity . . .

THE WIND

It blows like a hurricane coming in from the West.
Not a tree is spared, not even a nest.
Regardless of how strong and tough they stand,
The trees get little rest.
I've got to try to fight my way through the weather to pass the
    test.

THE MASTER'S REPLY

Son, nature must take its turn,
From winter to spring, one must always learn
The weak will fall and no longer stand tall.
While the babes in the woods won't be bothered at all.
Look to your faith to see you through and watch your step to
    avoid a fall.

THOSE NOT COMING HOME

Lord, oh Lord, what have we done.

Thousands upon thousands killed before the setting of the sun.

How many wives, husbands, sons, and daughters will no longer
see it rise?

Why hast Thee created such a lethal demise?

Show me, oh Lord, show me, what is the final prize?

THE MASTER'S REPLY

My son, it is not in war that one finds peace,

But rather in helping one another across the borders, to the
very least.

Offer happiness, joy, and a future to all left behind, regardless
of kind!

And treat them all the same when you say 'goodbye' . . .

My Father and I leave no one behind. We offer hope and prayer
to all mankind.

WEALTH OR FAITH

Lord, this is the Big One. I've found it at last
All the wealth I've desired and an open door to the upper class!
Oh, it takes a lie here or there to come true,
But I'm sure if anyone understands, it would be You.

THE MASTER'S REPLY

My son, fool not thyself.
The end of life is not measured in wealth.
Truth, justice, honesty, and faith will guide you to the eternal
place,
Where you'll see Me and your loved ones as well.
Don't sell yourself short and end up in Hell!

WHERE IS THE REWARD

My life is spent and none of it I repent.
Where's my reward in dollars and cents?
It seems so futile and lacking in sense.
As each goes by, I feel more tired and tense.

THE MASTER'S REPLY

My son, my son, your time is nearly done.
Very soon will finally come the last setting of the sun.
Until that time, enjoy and maintain your run!
But never forget to help others and share your fun.
The rewards of life are intended for all, not a few chosen some.

WORK TWO JOBS

Lord, tell me why I must work two jobs to make it go,
While my former counterpart is in the happy lane, living easy
    and slow.
Where did I go wrong, what did I do?
I thought I raised my family the best I could in the red, white,
    and blue!
My children are happy and learning well the ABCs,
While I'm working day and night nearly ruining my knees.
Tell me, Lord, what should I do.
I truly don't have a clue!

THE MASTER'S REPLY

My daughter, have you thought of prayer, however you'd like.
It need not be formal or the 15 decades in all.
Any form of prayer will do, short or tall.
Through prayer, doors will open and opportunities abound.
You have my blessings and comfort with each word you sound.
    Amen

www.ingramcontent.com/pod-product-compliance
Lightning Source LLC
Chambersburg PA
CBHW071738020426

42331CB00008B/2074